Drawing and Learning About Bugs

Using Shapes and Lines

by
Amy Bailey Muehlenhardt

Thanks to our advisers for their expertise, research, and advice:

Gary A. Dunn, M.S., Director of Education
Young Entomologists' Society
Lansing, Michigan

Susan Kesselring, M.A., Literacy Educator
Rosemount-Apple Valley-Eagan (Minnesota) School District

PICTURE WINDOW BOOKS
Minneapolis, Minnesota

Amy Bailey Muehlenhardt
grew up in Fergus Falls, Minnesota,
and attended Minnesota State
University in Moorhead. She holds
a Bachelor of Science degree in
Graphic Design and Art Education.
Before coming to Picture Window
Books, Amy was an elementary art
teacher. She always impressed upon
her students that "everyone is an artist."
Amy lives in Mankato, Minnesota,
with her husband, Brad.

To my nephews, Christian and Andrew—
we all love you so much.
To my Waconia students—every time you solve
a problem, you are thinking like an artist.
Be creative, and keep drawing!

ABM

Managing Editor: Bob Temple
Creative Director: Terri Foley
Editor: Sara E. Hoffmann
Editorial Adviser: Andrea Cascardi
Designer: Amy Bailey Muehlenhardt
Page production: Picture Window Books
The illustrations in this book were drawn with pencil.

Picture Window Books
5115 Excelsior Boulevard
Suite 232
Minneapolis, MN 55416
1-877-845-8392
www.picturewindowbooks.com

Printed in the United States of America.

Library of Congress Cataloging-in-Publication Data
Muehlenhardt, Amy Bailey, 1974-
Drawing and learning about bugs : using shapes and lines /
by Amy Bailey Muehlenhardt.
p. cm. — (Sketch it!)
Summary: Provides instructions for using simple shapes
and lines to draw insects.
Includes bibliographical references.
ISBN 1-4048-0270-3 (Reinforced Library Binding)
1. Insects in art—Juvenile literature.
2. Drawing—Technique—Juvenile literature. [1. Insects in art.
2. Drawing—Technique.] I. Title: Bugs. II. Title.
NC783 .M84 2004
743.6'57—dc22

2003019274

Table of Contents

Everyone Is an Artist
There is no right or wrong way to draw!

With a little patience and some practice, anyone can learn to draw. Did you know every picture begins as a simple shape? If you can draw shapes, you can draw anything.

The Basics of Drawing

line—a long mark made by a pen, a pencil, or another tool

guideline—a line used to help you draw. The guideline will be erased when your drawing is almost complete.

shade—to color in with your pencil

value—the lightness or darkness of an object

shape—the form or outline of an object or figure

diagonal—a shape or line that leans to the side

Before you begin, you will need:

a pencil
an eraser
lots of paper

Four Tips for Drawing

1. Draw very lightly.
To see how this is done, try drawing soft, medium, and dark lines. The softer you press, the lighter the lines will be.

2. Draw your shapes.
Connect them with a dark, sketchy line.

3. Add details.
Details are small things that make a good picture even better.

4. Smudge your art.
Use your finger to rub your lines. This will soften your picture and add shadows.

Let's get started!

Simple shapes help you draw.

Practice drawing these shapes before you begin:

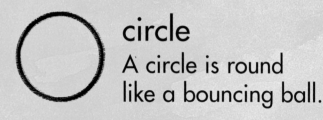 **circle**
A circle is round like a bouncing ball.

 **triangle**
A triangle has three sides and three corners.

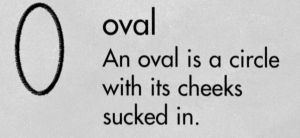 **oval**
An oval is a circle with its cheeks sucked in.

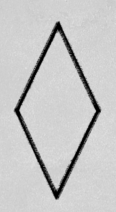 **diamond**
A diamond is two triangles put together.

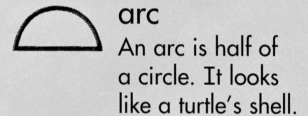 **arc**
An arc is half of a circle. It looks like a turtle's shell.

 **square**
A square has four equal sides and four corners.

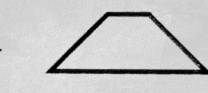 **trapezoid**
A trapezoid has four sides and four corners. Two of its sides are different lengths.

 **crescent**
A crescent looks like a banana.

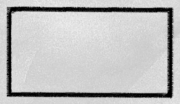 **rectangle**
A rectangle has two long sides, two short sides, and four corners.

You will also use lines when drawing.

Practice drawing these lines:

| vertical
A vertical line
stands tall like
a tree.

 zig zag
A zig-zag line is
sharp and pointy.

___ horizontal
A horizontal line
lies down and
takes a nap.

 wavy
A wavy line moves
up and down like
a roller coaster.

Remember to practice drawing.

While using this book, you may
want to stop drawing at step five
or six. That's great! Everyone is at
a different drawing level.

diagonal
A diagonal line
leans to the side.

Don't worry if your picture isn't
perfect. The important thing is
to have fun. You may wish to
add details to your drawing.
Does your bug crawl in a garden?
What color is your bug?
Create a background.

 dizzy
A dizzy line
spins around
and around.

Be creative!

Ant

Ants are tiny workers with different jobs. Ants find food, dig tunnels, and even become soldiers. Ants work hard all through the summer. When winter comes, ants hide in warm spots deep in the earth. An ant has three sections: the head, the thorax, and the abdomen.

Step 1

Draw a circle for the head. Draw a circle for the eye. Add two curved lines for antennae.

Step 2

Draw an oval for the thorax.

Step 3

Draw a larger circle for the abdomen. Add a triangle for the end tip of the abdomen.

Step 4

Draw three zig-zag lines for the legs on the near side. Draw all three legs in the middle section.

Step 5

Draw three zig-zag lines for the legs on the far side. They should match the legs you've already drawn on the near side.

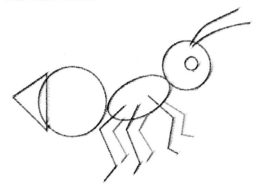

Step 6

Draw a curved line for the mouth. Trace over your lines and make them darker. Erase any lines you no longer need.

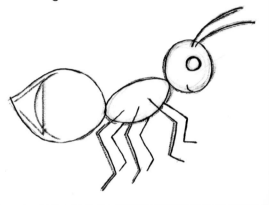

Step 7

Shade in the body with your pencil. Make the eye a darker shade than the rest of the ant.

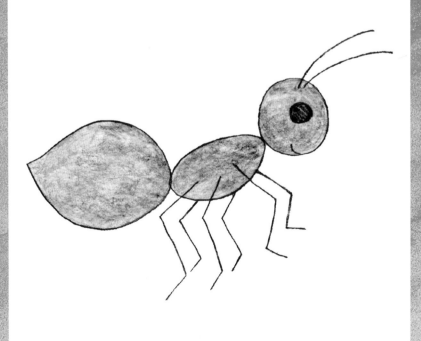

Dragonfly

Dragonflies live in warm climates. They are usually found near ponds and rivers. Dragonflies are very large. A full-grown dragonfly can be as large as an adult's hand!

Step 1
Draw a vertical guideline. This line will be erased. On the vertical guideline, draw an oval for the top part of the body.

Step 2
Draw an oval and a small circle for the head.

Step 3
Draw an oval for the bottom part of the body. Divide the oval on the top into two circles for the eyes. Add zig-zag lines for the arms.

Step 4
Below the head, draw four ovals for the wings. Two ovals will be on each side of the body.

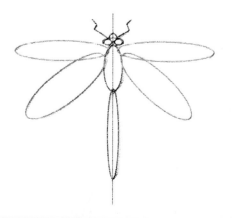

Step 5

Trace over the lines you want to keep.

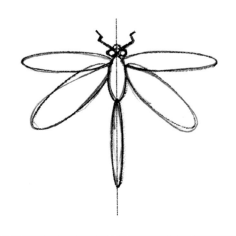

Step 6

Begin shading in the body. Leave some areas white for markings. Erase the lines you no longer need.

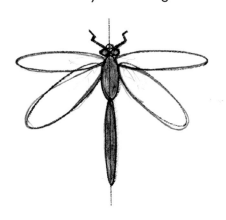

Step 7

Continue shading and add thin lines to the wings. Leave some areas white for markings.

Grasshopper

The largest grasshopper can jump a distance of six feet (1.8 meters). Grasshoppers rub their long back legs together to make noise. These insects eat plants of all kinds.

Step 1

Draw an oval for the body. Overlap the oval with a square for the neck.

Step 2

Draw an oval for the head. Add a small circle for the eye. Draw two curved lines for the antennae.

Step 3

Draw two zig-zag lines for the front legs. Draw two more zig-zag lines for the middle legs.

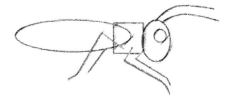

Step 4

Draw two large zig-zag lines for the back legs.

Step 5

Draw a horizontal line across the oval for the wings. Repeat the zig-zag lines for the front, middle, and back legs, making the legs thick.

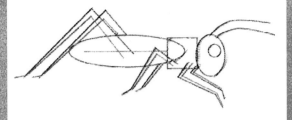

Step 6

Trace over the lines you want to keep. Add a curved line for the mouth. Erase the lines you no longer need.

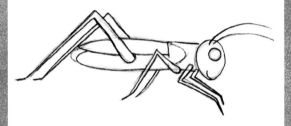

Step 7

Shade in the grasshopper using your pencil. Make the eye darker.

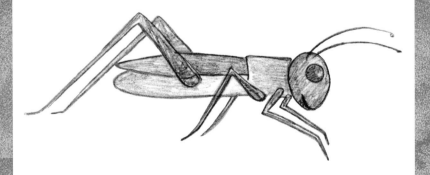

Ladybug

Ladybugs are a type of beetle. They are usually orange with black spots. Ladybugs keep plants healthy by getting rid of pests in the garden.

Step 1

Draw a circle for the body. Draw a vertical line down the center of the circle.

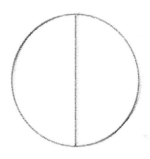

Step 2

Draw an oval for the head. Add two circles and a rectangle on the top of the head.

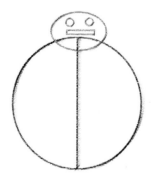

Step 3

Draw two curved lines for antennae.

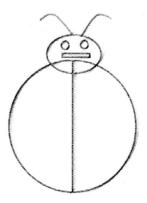

Step 4

Draw six short zig-zag lines for legs. A ladybug has three legs on each side.

Step 5

Draw different-sized circles for spots on the body.

Step 6

Trace over the lines you want to keep. Erase the lines you no longer need. Begin shading with your pencil.

Step 7

Continue shading in the head, body, and spots. The spots on the ladybug's head should be lighter than the spots on its body. Darken the legs.

Monarch Butterfly

A monarch butterfly lays its eggs on the underside of milkweed plant leaves. Caterpillars hatch from the eggs and begin feeding on the plant. A caterpillar sheds its skin and creates a chrysalis. A monarch comes from the chrysalis.

Step 1

Draw a small circle for the head. Draw two curved lines with rounded ends for antennae.

Step 2

Draw an oval for the top section of the body. Draw a longer oval for the bottom section of the body.

Step 3

Draw two long, curved lines for the wings. Start the lines between the circle and the oval.

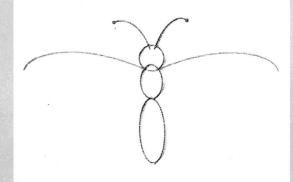

Step 4

Draw wavy lines down to the bottom of the long oval. The lines should curve like the top of a heart.

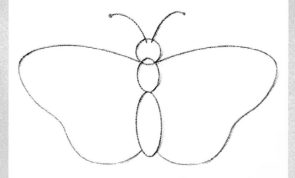

16

Step 5

Repeat the curved and wavy lines on the inside of the wing. Add a curved line like a rainbow across the wings.

Step 6

Add curved lines inside the wings for designs. Draw small circles for white spots on the wings, body, and head. Erase the lines you no longer need.

Step 7

Continue shading the butterfly. Make the outside edge of the wings darker. Leave the spots white.

Wasp

Wasps sting and kill insect pests. Wasps love to visit picnics and eat trash, such as rotten fruit. Wasps are black and yellow.

Step 1

Draw a circle for the smaller part of the body.

Step 2

Draw an oval for the head.
Draw a large circle for the eye.
Add two curved lines for antennae.

Step 3

Draw a larger oval for the larger part of the body.

Step 4

Draw two large ovals for the wings.

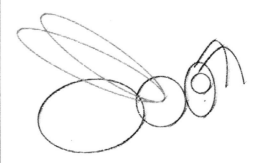

Step 5

Draw three zig-zag lines for the legs. Start drawing the zig-zag lines at the middle circle.

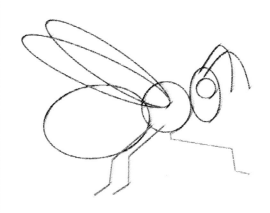

Step 6

Trace over the lines. Erase half of the wing on the far side. Erase the lines you no longer need.

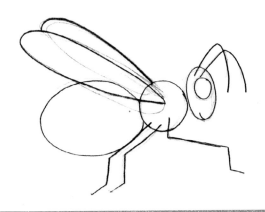

Step 7

Add curved lines for stripes on the end section of the body. Make a pattern by shading in the stripes. Continue shading. Add thin wing lines.

Bedbug

Bedbugs have flat bodies and are reddish-brown. They can live for months without food. Bedbugs live in warm, dry places. They bite birds, bats, dogs, and even people!

Step 1

Draw a medium-sized circle for the middle section of the bedbug.

Step 2

Draw a small circle for the head.

Step 3

Draw a larger oval for the back section of the body. The oval and the middle circle should overlap.

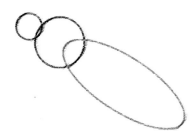

Step 4

Draw two diagonal lines for the legs on each side of the oval. Add short lines for the feet.

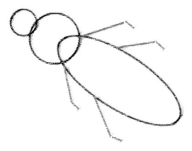

Step 5

Add two diagonal lines for the arms. Add short lines for the hands. Draw two curved lines for the antennae.

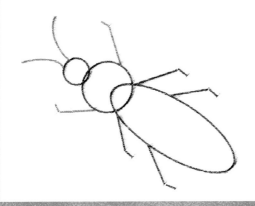

Step 6

Trace over the lines. When tracing, curve the middle circle like the letter C. Sketch a pointed tip at the end of the oval for the body. Erase the lines you no longer need.

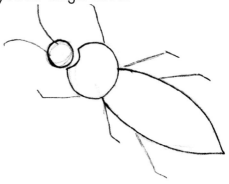

Step 7

Continue to darken the lines. Shade in the bedbug with your pencil. Shade the head darker than the rest of the body. Add a point on the head for the beak.

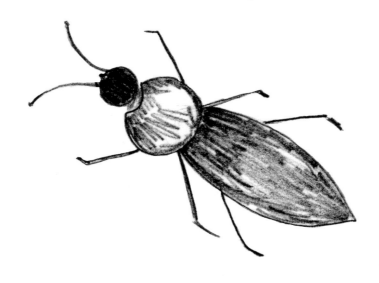

Pond Skater

Pond skaters walk on the surface of the water. They are very light. A pond skater's body has a protective coat of fur on it to keep the water away. The fur is so thin you can't see it.

Step 1

Draw a long, skinny oval for the body. Draw a small rectangle for the head.

Step 2

At the bottom of the rectangle, add two circles for the eyes. Draw two curved lines for antennae.

Step 3

Draw six zig-zag lines for the legs. Four of the legs begin at the oval. Two of the legs begin at the rectangle head.

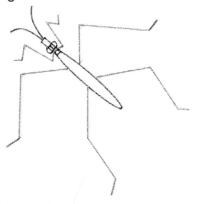

Step 4

Draw short lines across the end of the long oval.

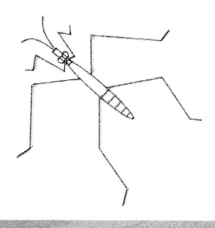

Step 5

Draw thin circles around each foot to show the water.

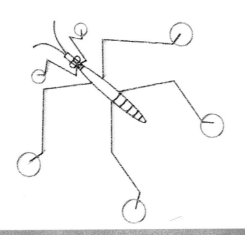

Step 6

Trace over the lines you want to keep. Erase the lines you no longer need.

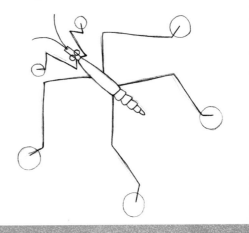

Step 7

Shade in the pond skater using the side of your pencil.

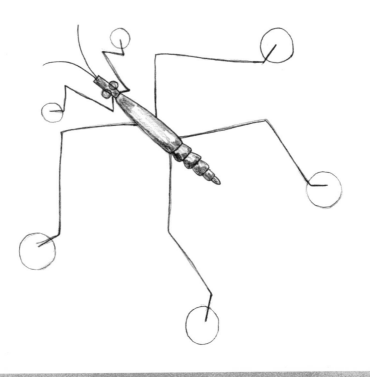

To Learn More

At the Library

Kistler, Mark. *Dare to Draw in 3-D: Cartoon Critters.* New York: Scholastic, 2002.

Loewen, Nancy. *Living Lights: Fireflies in Your Backyard.* Minneapolis: Picture Window Books, 2004.

Randolph, Joanne. *Let's Draw a Butterfly with Circles.* New York: PowerKids Press, 2004.

VanCleave, Janice Pratt. *Janice VanCleave's Play and Find Out About Bugs: Easy Experiments for Young Children.* New York: J. Wiley, 1999.

Walsh, Ellen Stoll. *Dot & Jabber and the Big Bug Mystery.* Orlando: Harcourt, 2003.

On the Web

Fact Hound

Fact Hound offers a safe, fun way to find Web sites related to this book. All of the sites on Fact Hound have been researched by our staff. http://www.facthound.com

1. Visit the Fact Hound home page.
2. Enter a search word related to this book, or type in this special code: 1404802703.
3. Click on the FETCH IT button.

Your trusty Fact Hound will fetch the best sites for you!